The Love of a Tree

Isis Bingham

BookLeaf
Publishing

India | USA | UK

Presentation by *BookLeaf Publishing*

Web: www.bookleafpub.com

E-mail: info@bookleafpub.com

ISBN: 9789360942199

First edition 2024

*To my friends who never stopped believing
in me*

Sonder

I step on the bus
Taking my seat
I see a man nodding his head
To music playing in his headphones
I wonder if it's his favorite song
And how many times it's been replayed

Walking down the street
I see a lady with a tattoo
A name with angel wings
The skin around it red and puffy
I wonder if she lost a family member recently

Passing through a town
I see a rundown local diner
And wonder if
It was someone's favorite place once

Strangers I only see in passing
Never to be seen again
Sometimes I forget that
Strangers are also people

Broken Windows

2

They say that
Eyes are windows to the soul
Don't look into mine
Broken and dull
I want to put curtains up
Want to hide myself from the world
I'm scared of people seeing me
And seeing how shattered I am

River Chorus

Water runs over
Rocks and stones, singing softly
In the quiet woods

Dear God

Dear God
Can you hear me?
I'm sorry it's been a while
I've been lost and trying to find a way
On my own
But I can't do it without you
Dear God
Are you there?
Sometimes I feel like you're not
How can there be a God
In this fallen world?
Dear God
Please help me
Pick me up to my feet
And give me the strength
To keep going
Dear God
I'm trying
Please don't forsake me
Teach me
To love again

Dancing Alone

I pull up our favorite songs
With all our favorite memories
I see the candlelight flickering
And feel your hand against my waist
The first song plays, and we sway to the music
The melody rises and fades out
With it the image of you is gone
And I was dancing alone

Reflection

I look into the mirror
Eyes tracing over every flaw
Every scar and stretch mark
The asymmetry of my face
I want to cover myself
Hide my ugly imperfections
But then your voice comes to me
Reminds me of the stories
Behind each mark
And that I'm beautiful
Through every scar

A Foggy Morning

There's nothing quite like
A foggy morning
When the world is still asleep
The sunshine rays
Softly pierce the sky, carving
Into the mist
The fog swirls around me
In whirling pools
And cradles me so gently
The birds sing
A sweet lilting tune, echoing
Through the trees
And fills me with calming peace

How Dare You

How dare you say "I love you"
After hurting me like that
How dare you say "I'm sorry"
When you turn around right back
How dare you doubt me
After all I've given you
How dare you ask more of me
When I've already sacrificed so much

Running On Empty

The engine light is on in my head
But I keep pushing on
The gas is running on empty
But I don't have time to eat
People tell me to slow down
But my brake lines are cut
And I'm spinning out of control

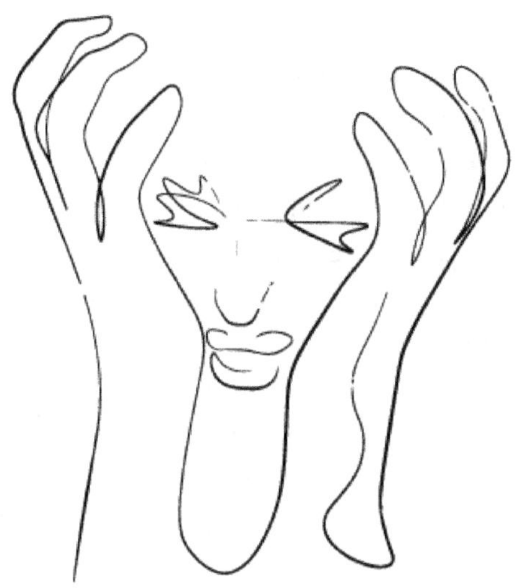

Love like a Tree

True love is like a tree.
When the winds beat down on the sapling
The roots grow deeper
Grasping firmly to the ground
Unmovable and unshakable.

When the bough and trunk bend
The bark grows thicker
Shielding the soft wood
Unbendable and unbreakable.

True love is like a tree
When the hard times come
It adapts to the circumstance
So that when those times pass
It comes out stronger for it.

True love is like a tree
In time as it matures
It grows strong and bears fruit
Sweet and filling to the soul.

Beachside

Ocean waves crash against the land
Water rippling across my toes
My footprints leaving traces in the sand
I watch the sun set
Painting the beachside in colors grand

Greener Grass

The saying goes:
The grass is greener
On the other side.
Makes people always looking
Over the other side of the fence.
But the grass is greener
Where you water it.
Choose, then
If you will water what's yours
Or chase after your neighbor's
Leaving your grass
Brown and dead

Self-Love

The most important thing
Is having self-love
Love in yourself builds
Trust and confidence
That when times are tough
You can come out on top
Love from friends is good
But some friends leave
Love from family is well
But they've got their demons, too
You can never leave yourself
Wherever you go,
Your shadow follows
So love yourself
And come out the champion

Cherry Blossoms

There's a cherry tree in my backyard
It blooms every mid-spring
Light pink flowers covering the branches
When the wind passes through
It sends the blossoms flying
Filling the air with snow in April

Text Message

I check my phone
Once, twice, a third time
Waiting for a text from you
Filled with anticipation
To talk to you
And when my phone lights up
With a notification from you
I smile giddily
Happy to be talking to you

Round and Around

I feel stuck
Like the end of a record track
Spinning round and around
I can't get out of
Making the same mistakes
I guess I got used to the sound
Of the static
Not knowing how to get up
Pick myself off the ground
Someone help me
Pull me out of this rut
Help me be found

Find You

The rain falls from the sky, it falls on my face,
Masking the tears
Thunder rumbles, covering my cries,
Crying for you.
Why did you leave me?
Where can I find you?
On the grass, catching my tears,
In the wind, brushing my hair
In the sun, waiting to feed the flowers
After the rain has fallen

Up All Night

I lie in my bed
Tossing and turning
I check my clock
Only five minutes have passed
Since the last time I looked
My thoughts spin in my head
Keeping me up all night
Wishing I could say to you
All the words I want to say
Wishing I could change
All the mistakes I've made
I stay up all night
Ruminating and reminiscing
I check my clock again
Three minutes had passed

Last Breath

My greatest wish is
To take my last breath in bed
With you at my side

Sound of Rain

Dripping raindrops
Pound the roof
Creates a soothing rhythm
Soothes me to sleep
And brings me memories of you

Dripping raindrops
Pattering on leaves
Rivulets pouring like tears
Like how we cried that day
Holding each other tightly

Dripping raindrops
Beating the ground
Smell of wet earth strong
Like the cologne you wore
Enveloping me in your embrace

Dripping raindrops
Clattering the windows
Fogging up the glass
Like our breath in the cold
Walking together in the rain

Dripping raindrops
Sound of rain
Music of nature
A comforting lullaby
Full of memories of you

All In

In this game of life
I keep my cards close to my chest
Careful to keep my poker face
I want to play my best
Knowing when I should fold
Or when I risk the rest
And go all in

Burn the Memories

I strike the match
Igniting a small flame
A pile in front of me
Photographs and souvenirs
Of memories too painful to remember
I've tried so hard to forget
The pain that came when you left
But I've been holding on
To those memories
Through the photos and trinkets
I want to be free of it
Free of the pain
So I have to let it burn

Good Old Days

I remember when
We stayed out til dark
And the street lights turned on
We raced each other on bikes
And ate popsicles off the back porch
When all our worries were just
Homework and household chores
Now it's bills and mortgages
Rundown cars and long work hours
I remember when we laughed
And smiled without a care
Wish we could go back
To the good old days

Mother's Arms

At the end of a long day
There's nothing I love more
Than to curl up in mother's arms
To have her kiss my cheek
And softly stroke my hair
There's no other feeling
Like being held by Mother
By the one who gave me life
And who sacrificed everything for me
When times are hard
And I need solace
I fall into Mother's embrace
And wish I could stay there
Forever

My Own Shadow

Some days I feel like I'm not in control
Flipped the switch to airplane mode
I'm awake but not running the show
Just following myself around
Like I'm my own shadow

Thunderstorm

Dark clouds gathering
Winds pick up and rain falls as
Blinding lights flicker

Springtime

In the dead of winter
Knee-high with snow
I can't help but wish
For the sun's soft glow
Many barren trees
Left without their leaves
Leaves one wanting
For a warm spring breeze
The animals hide to sleep
Warm in their holes
I miss seeing
The rabbits and voles
The new world arrayed
In snow and in ice
I long for a time
When the weather is nice
Year after year
Every winter clime
I always wish and wait
For the joyous springtime

Haunted

I hope you know
That when I'm gone
My ghost will follow you
So that you'll never be alone

The End of the Tunnel

The road's been long
The journey hard
Traveling alone and in the dark
My feet ache from the walk
Sometimes I want
To slow down and stop
But I keep pressing on
Because I know
Eventually
I'll come to the finish
And see the light
At the end of the tunnel

Voicemail

I'm sorry I missed your call
I was sleeping
And my phone on silent
When I woke up and saw
Three missed calls from you
I tried calling you back
In a panic
Thinking something was wrong
You didn't pick up
Please tell me you're ok
Call me back as soon as possible

Slow Dance

Soft music playing in the background
Your hand pressed against my back
Our bodies swaying from side to side
I lean my head against your shoulder
And dance the night away with you

Tossed In the Wind

Winds blowing, thunder rolling
Waves crashing down
A boat in the ocean
Tips up and down in the fray
A lighthouse in the distance
Shines a beacon as a warning
Guiding the boat from rocky shores
Keeling in the storm, tossed in the wind

Aurora Borealis

The perfect night, a clear dark sky
An empty canvas for a watchful eye
Slowly flickering, a misty flame
Colorful lights of otherworldly fame
Twirling and swirling, making a dance
Blues and greens in a trance
The color swells, bursting in air
Then fades away quickly to disappear

Sleep Tight

I hold you tight
Your eyes drooping close
I rock you back and forth
Sleep tight
"I'm not tired"
You tell me
But I know it's a lie
Just rest, my dear
Sleep tight
"I'm wide awake"
You say, fighting a yawn
I laugh softly
And kiss your cheek
Sleep tight
Your eyes are closed
There's a gentle snore
A dream filled pillow
Sleep tight

Autumn

Hues of red and orange
Crisp leaves falling from the trees
Covering the ground

My Best Friend

My best friend
Brings out the best in me
Highlights my talents
Balances my flaws
Encourages me to reach for the stars
I wouldn't be anywhere
Without my best friend

Forget

I tried so hard to hold on
But you didn't want to
You up and left
Took everything with you
Now I'm left alone
After all we'd been through
How can you expect
Me to forget you

A Future With You

I love your eyes
Your hair, your smile
I love your laugh
And every freckle you despise
When I'm in your arms
I feel safe
Warm and protected
You know every piece of me
And I know you
When we're together
I feel loved and complete
Like I found a part of me
I didn't know I was missing
I want to be like this forever
Wake up every day
With you by my side
Because I know
When you're with me
I can do anything
As long as I have
A future with you

Abandoned Dreams

When I was a little child
I looked at the stars and wished
To go travel the vast seas
To be a renowned scientist
To cure a deadly disease
To do something worth remembering
Now I am older
Caught in the mundane day-to-day
Wishing I'd caught those dreams
Now forgotten to yesterday

Lost to Time

41

Ivy vines curl up marble statues
Rust covers the iron gates
Weeds grow in the long grass
A garden overgrown and neglected
Its caretakers had long since abandoned
Leaving wild nature to run its course

Little Crescent Moon

42

Little crescent moon up in the sky
Shining brightly
Light my path as I go to sleep
Dreaming moondust
Protect me as I travel to distant lands
Sleeping soundly
Little crescent moon behind drifting clouds
Blinding white
Guide my steps from foreign shores
Little crescent moon

Cruising

Windows rolled down
Music turned up
We're cruising down the highway
Wind blows through my hair
I smile at you
Hand drifting up and down in the breeze
Just me, you, and this song
Cruising down the highway

Found

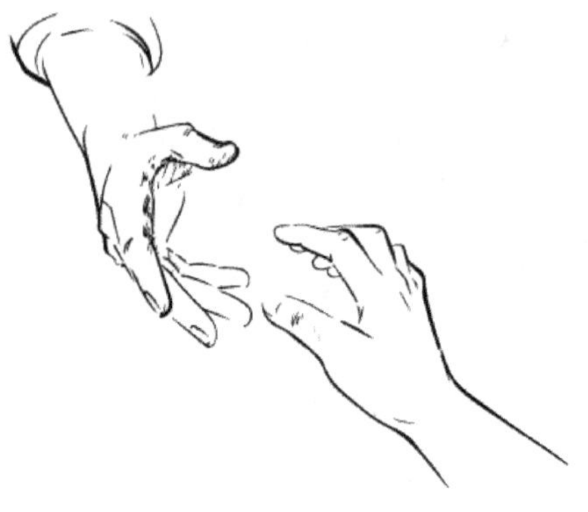

I kneel in the dark
Curled up small
I've wandered for so long
I don't know where I am
Falling deeper in despair
The darkness creeps around me
Feeling a chill in my bones
Wondering if I ever
Will find my way back again
Suddenly, a light shines in the dark
I look up and see
A hand reaching down
Pulling me back up

Going in Circles

45

Round and round I go
Making the same mistakes
Getting the same consequences
I try to change, to be someone new
But I feel like I'm going in circles
Running the same track
How can I get out of this rut
Without going back?

Little Child

She hands me her baby
My sweet little cousin
I take you in my arms
And hold you gently close
I have no children of my own
And yet, holding you, I know
Why mothers fight tooth and nail
To protect their little ones
Little child, you are precious to me

The Person I Fell in Love With

The person I fell in love with
Is not the person I love now
Some change is good, it makes us strong
But I've seen you change, how
Is it that you've changed so much
I hardly recognize you now
You've broken my heart, my trust
You've broken every single vow
I tried so hard to understand you
To work through every row
But I've come to terms that the one I love
Isn't the same person now

Thank You, Mother

The one who raised me, provided me a home
Who taught me everything I know
You picked me up after every fall
And wiped away my tears
Your advice I always needed,
Though I didn't always follow
You helped me through my sorrow
And calmed all my fears
Your sacrifice I can never repay

Foot Race

Running, running, running
Trying to keep in pace
I see people passing by
I'm trying to stay in the race

Running, running, running
Now I'm falling behind
Getting tired of keeping up
Now I'm just running blind

Running, running, running
Feet and legs are aching
No end in sight
And my motivation is shaking

Waterfall

50

Pouring over the
Edge of the cliff, rushing and
Pounding like a drum

Secrets

Some things are better left unsaid
Better to be hidden in my head
Things I'd rather not have people know
Rather not let those feelings show
I care what others think of me
Need to make sure they can't see
Keep those secrets safe and sound
Somewhere where they can't be found

Words Leave Scars

52

The power of words is a fickle thing
Things intangible, but yet
They leave marks on us, forever impressed
In our souls
A kind word, a warm glow in the bosom
A harsh word, a cut in the mind
The things we say, we mostly don't think
One careless slip and we've thrown a knife
Invisible scars

Blank Pages

A new day, new dawn
A fresh start, blank page
Whatever's past can't be rewritten
Nor can it be erased
Nothing is important now
But the writing on the new page
As many days as you live
Is as many as you can start over
A new day, new dawn
A fresh start, blank page

Snow

54

Little cold flakes like
Downy feathers floating down
Blanketing the ground

Never Say Goodbye

I never say goodbye
It just sounds too final
Like I'm never going to return
I promise I'll come right back

Choked On Weeds

When I was younger
And more naive,
I thought myself the Master Gardener.

Your love was the crop
And mine was the soil.

I tilled and watered,
And the garden flowered
And bloomed.

But I failed to notice,
In my inexpertise,

The flowers were thistles
And creeping vines

And poison ivy.

I thought it was love
I was growing.

But I
Choked
On those weeds.

Star Bright

Star light, star bright,
First star I see tonight,
Wish I may, wish I might
Have the wish I wish tonight.

Star bright in the sky,
Oh how I wish to fly.
Wish I may, wish I try
Far above the view of eye.

Star bright, my far away friend,
Hope to me please send.
Wish I may, wish I mend,
Bring this sadness to an end.

Star bright, beautiful star,
Shining light from afar,
Wish I may, wish in a jar,
To be right where you are.

As You Are

59

You hide,
Scared to show me
Your scars.
You look away,
Ashamed to show me
Your tears.
You swallow your voice,
Afraid to show me
Your mind.

Darling,
Do not hide from me.
Do not turn away
Nor silence yourself.
Do not make yourself small
In hopes to be more palatable.

Darling,
I love you as you are,
And if the world cannot love
You as you are,
Let me be your world.

Chasm

I gave you my heart
I loved every part of you
I felt whole with you
Now you're gone
Rug pulled from under my feet
And all that's left
Is a chasm where you were
In my heart

Chipped Away

To my beloved
I divide my soul
I carve out pieces
With each touch
Each breath
Every cry and every laugh
I tear myself apart
Give myself
I chip
Chip
Chip myself away
Til my whole soul
Is theirs

Look to the Moon

When I am gone
Look to the moon
See my smile reflected
In its crescent shape.

When I'm not here
Look to the stars
See my eyes sparkle
In their twinkling dance.

When you miss me
Look to the ocean
Hear my laugh ring
In their crashing waves.

When you need me
Turn to the wind
Feel my embrace caress
In its passing touch.

When we are apart
Turn to the sun
And know that I
Am always with you
In your heart

Starcrossed

I never understood why
women wanted
A Romeo
When his story was
A tragedy
A doomed narrative.
Then I met you
And I understood.
Not all at once
But slowly
Our passion took over
All forms of reason.
I loved you so vibrantly
That I willingly
Took
That poison vial.
We were star-crossed lovers
But a star-crossed love
Never seems a tragedy
Until Juliet wakes up
And sees the empty
Vial in Romeo's
Cold hand.

Birdsong

I wake up to the
symphony
Of trilling birds
I wish to have your
Company
The beautiful whistles
And sing-song warbles of
Simplicity
Cause me to
Miss you, and my
Fantasy
Is that wherever you are
The same birdsong
Harmony
Is playing to you
My darling

The Most Dangerous Thing

Sticks and stones may
break my bones
Glass may shatter and knives
Cut my skin
And poison may
kill my body
But these don't compare
The most dangerous thing
Is to give your heart away
To love most ardently
You see, sticks and stones,
Glass and knives,
And poison
They all bring pain
But the pain has an end
The scars eventually heal
Even death
Brings a certain solace
But to love is the most
Dangerous thing
Because to love is to risk
Everything
Trusting a piece of your soul
To another and hoping
That they don't break you

And if they break you
That pain can never heal
That trust can never mend
The scars will never go away
The most dangerous thing
Is to love
Because when you find someone
To love
That longing can easily turn
To bitterness and spite
And a heart is too easily
Bruised

One Last Time

Had I known you'd be gone
I would have hugged you
A little tighter
I would have stared into your eyes
A little deeper
If I had known I wouldn't see you
That kiss would have been
A little longer
I would have whispered in your ear
Over and over and over again
I love you, my darling
That Polaroid photo
you wanted for your wallet
I would have taken it
Now that you're gone
And I'm all alone
I'm filled with regrets
Thinking maybe I hadn't
Loved you hard enough
That I hadn't cherished you
Sufficiently the way you deserved
Had I known the sword
Was going to fall so soon
I would have done so many things
And I would give

Anything
To see you
One last time

Little Death

They say dying is easy
Living is harder
But why separate the two
And make life the martyr?
The two are so
Intrinsically tied
That where one goes
The other can't hide
A day of joy
Will turn to sadness
A day of peace
Turns into madness
To live is to experience
The little Death
The tiny travesties
That steals my breath
The loss of a friend
The wilt of a flower
All of it says
I have no power
There is no escape
From the little Death

Roots

Small tendrils in the
Ground keeping me stable and
Secure where I am

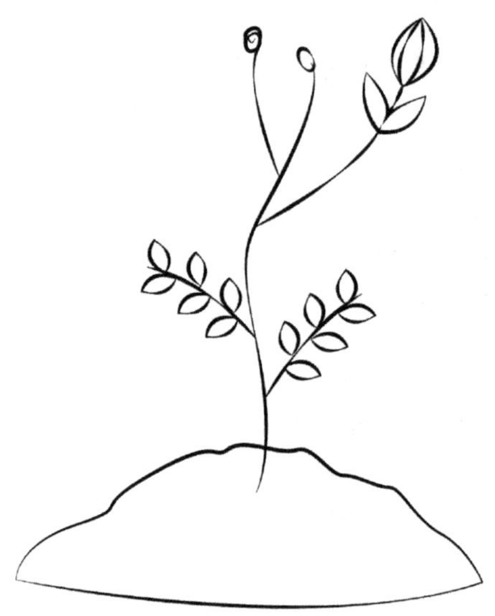

Skydive

High up in the air
Earth far below
And nothing in between
But the air bitter cold
I tremble with fear
Afraid of the fall
The lack of stability
Holds me still
I tremble to think
Of the plummet down
To spin out and crash
I wait many moments
Gathering strength then
With a spark of courage
Eyes clenched shut
I jump into the dive
Feeling weightless
And free

Eternal

When times are hard
Or when I feel sad
I write those things
Down in the sand

When times are good
Or when I feel glad
I write those things
Down in stone

The sand will shift
From winds and the waves
And the things I wrote
Will eventually fade

The stone is hard
And resists the passing of time
And the things I wrote
Will always stay

And when I am old
And reflect back on life
The only thing I see
Is my happiness eternal

Astronaut

Your eyes
Like supernovas
Pull me in
Like gravity
Wherever you walk
There's a trail
Of stardust
Guiding me to you
Your smile
Like the sun
Warm and bright
What could I do
Without your light?
My love for you
Is as deep
And vast
As the infinite
Expanse of space
I follow you
Wherever you go
I am your
Astronaut
Weightless in
Your embrace

White Lies

74

"I'm fine", I say,
avoiding your gaze
"It's nothing",
clenching hands behind my back
"No need to worry"

I want to protect you from my sadness
I hug you, hiding tears in my eyes
That's why I tell you
These little white lies

Easy Come

I found you so easily
We fell into each other
Like magnets put together
I enjoyed every moment with you

Til the cracks started
And the chill set in
I tried to plaster up the breaks
And warm you with my heart

Easy come, easy go
They say
But it's a lie
For as easily as you came to me
It was hard to let you go
Like ripping two magnets apart